Gods and Goddesses

by Grace Hansen

Abdo Kids Jumbo is an Imprint of Abdo Kids
abdobooks.com

abdobooks.com

Published by Abdo Kids, a division of ABDO, P.O. Box 398166, Minneapolis, Minnesota 55439.

Printed in the United States of America, North Mankato, Minnesota.

102023

012024

Photo Credits: Alamy, Getty Images, Granger Collection, Shutterstock, ©British Museum p19 / CC BY-NC-SA 4.0

Production Contributors: Teddy Borth, Jennie Forsberg, Grace Hansen
Design Contributors: Victoria Bates, Candice Keimig

Library of Congress Control Number: 2023937697

Publisher's Cataloging-in-Publication Data

Names: Hansen, Grace, author.

Title: Gods and goddesses / by Grace Hansen

Description: Minneapolis, Minnesota : Abdo Kids, 2024 | Series: Discovering ancient Egypt | Includes online resources and index.

Identifiers: ISBN 9781098268442 (lib. bdg.) | ISBN 9781098269142 (ebook) | ISBN 9781098269494 (Read-to-Me ebook)

Subjects: LCSH: Gods, Egyptian--Juvenile literature. | Goddesses, Egyptian--Juvenile literature. | Divine beings--Juvenile literature.

Classification: DDC 932--dc23

Table of Contents

Powerful Gods

The ancient Egyptians did not understand the natural world. They did not know why the sun moved across the sky or why rain fell. They believed the gods controlled everything.

One of the most important gods to the ancient Egyptians was Ra. He was the sun god. He sailed across the sky each day. At night, he moved through the **underworld**.

Ra

The Egyptians believed that pharaohs were the god Horus in human form. Horus was the son of Osiris and Isis. He was king of the living, the earth, and the light.

Horus
Osiris
Isis

Isis was the **supreme** mother goddess. She helped people with childbirth, healing, and love. Ancient Egyptians also believed she protected them after death.

Osiris was the king of Egypt until his brother Seth killed him. Isis brought him back to life. Osiris became the god of the afterlife.

Osiris
Isis

Guided through the Afterlife

The afterlife was an important part of Egyptian religion. After a person died, the god Anubis led the spirit to the **Hall of Judgment**.

Anubis

Maat, the goddess of truth, was in the hall. She performed the Weighing of the Heart ceremony. Thoth, the god of writing, **recorded** the results.

Thoth
Maat

If the dead person's heart was heavier than a feather, they failed. Their heart was fed to the goddess Ammit. The person's spirit would no longer exist.

Ammit

If the dead person's heart was lighter than a feather, they had led a good life. Anubis would take the spirit to the Field of Reeds. Osiris ruled this **paradise**.

Anubis
heart
feather

More Egyptian Gods

Atum

- the original god who brought forth the world
- created himself

Amun

- god of the air and king of the gods
- later merged with the sun god Ra

Shu

- god of peace, air, and wind

Tefnut

- goddess of moisture and rain

Geb

- god of the earth
- central to the ancient Egyptian creation myth

Nut

- goddess of the sky and heavens

Hathor

- goddess of beauty, music, love, and dancing
- protector of women

Seth

- god of chaos
- symbolized storms, droughts, hunger, and war

Glossary

Hall of Judgment – where souls of the dead travel to face Osiris and other gods to determine whether they lived a good life.

paradise – a place where good people go after death.

recorded – put in writing.

supreme – greatest; having the highest position.

underworld – also known as the *Duat*, the world of the afterlife where the dead roam. It is also home to several gods who help judge the dead.

Index

Visit **abdokids.com** to access crafts, games, videos, and more!

Use Abdo Kids code

DGK8442

or scan this QR code!